Learning
Sight Words
with Ease

Easy Learning Books

FOR

TREY, MORGAN AND LANGSTON

For best results for learning. Practice sight words daily. Teach words repetitively until they are mastered. Use sentences to reinforce sight word recognition.

I

can

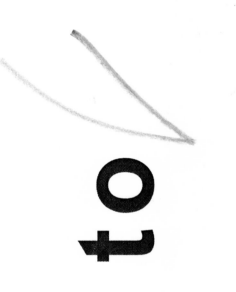

see

hat

CAt

You

pig

away

big

come

down

want

look

jump

make

me

at

play

red

run

said

we

us

stop

the

many

made

and

those

only

that

their

give

have

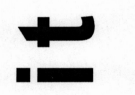

eat

he

her

with

try

sit

two

put

blue

funny

little

am

like

but

get

by

for

are

again

please

uncle

black

fly

take

dress

drink

pull

because

green

walk

small

much

long

work

sleep

buy

call

goes

better

wrong

grow

show

ate

far

sister

brother

father

mother

baby

bear

your

I see her.

Run with me.

Try to sit down.

He said jump.

I can see you.

Put those away.

Come to eat.

Look what he did.

I have to go.

We can play.

Don't look down.

Play with us.

It is red.

I made that.

Go with me.

I can jump.

Give it a try.

Sit those down.

Call your mother.

My brother can run.

Play with the baby.

The bear is little.

Ride with me.

Put that down.

Don't play with the bear.

Get in with me.

I like the bear.

I see your sister.

Printed in the United States
55989LVS00003B/4-33